GOOD NEWS

PRESCHOOL ACTIVITY BOOK

Lifeway Press®
Nashville, TN

EDITORIAL TEAM KIDS MINISTRY PUBLISHING

Chuck Peters
Director, Kids Ministry

Jeremy Carroll
Publishing Manager,
VBS and Kids Discipleship

Rhonda VanCleave
Publishing Team Leader

**Becky Suggs
Carol Tomlinson**
Writers

Klista Storts
Content Editor

Sara Lansford
Production Editor

Alli Quattlebaum
Graphic Designer

© Copyright 2022 Lifeway Press®

No part of this work may be reproduced or transmitted in any form or by any means, electronic or mechanical, including photocopying and recording, or by any information storage or retrieval system, except as may be expressly permitted in writing by the publisher.
Requests for permission should be addressed in writing to
Lifeway Press®
One Lifeway Plaza
Nashville, TN 37234

ISBN: 9781087766829
Item 005837991
Dewey Decimal Classification Number: 268.432
Subject Heading: Discipleship—Curricula\God\Bible—Study
Dewey Decimal Classification Number: 248.82
Subject Heading: CHRISTIAN LIFE \ JESUS CHRIST--TEACHINGS

Printed in the United States of America

Kids Ministry Publishing
Lifeway Church Resources
One Lifeway Plaza
Nashville, Tennessee 37234

We believe the Bible has God for its author; salvation for its end; and truth, without any mixture of error, for its matter and that all Scripture is totally true and trustworthy. To review Lifeway's doctrinal guideline, please visit lifeway.com/doctrinalguideline.

Unless otherwise indicated, all Scripture quotations are taken from the Christian Standard Bible®, Copyright © 2017 by Holman Bible Publishers. Used by permission. Christian Standard Bible® and CSB® are federally registered trademarks of Holman Bible Publishers.

TeamKID® is a registered trademark of Lifeway.

CONTENTS

1	The Promise	5
2	The Family	7
3	The Arrival	9
4	The Messenger	11
5	The Son	13
6	The Call	15
7	The Ministry Begins	17
8	The Kingdom of God	19
9	The Way to the Kingdom	21
10	The Healer	23
11	The Creator	25
12	The Forgiver	27
13	The Compassionate One	29
14	The Sender	31
15	The One to Come	33
16	The Lawgiver	35
17	The Sower	37
18	The Son of God	39
19	The Promised One	41
20	The Merciful Neighbor	43
21	The Lost Are Found	45
22	The First Are Last	47
23	The Poor Are Rich	49
24	The Generous King	51
25	The Kingdom Is for Everyone	53
26	The Rewards of the Kingdom	55
27	Waiting for the Kingdom	57
28	The Anointing	59
29	The King	61
30	The Last Supper	63
31	God's Kingdom Has Come	65
32	The King of Kings	67
33	The Promise Kept	69
34	The Promise Fulfilled	71
35	The Restoration	73
36	The Promise Continued	75
Bonus Session 1	Who Is Jesus?	77
Bonus Session 2	The Shepherds Worshiped Jesus	79
Bonus Session 3	Jesus Is Alive	81
Bonus Session 4	The Mission of the Kingdom	83

Parents & Families,

Thank you for giving us the opportunity to work with your preschooler in TeamKID! TeamKID is a fun, high-energy ministry that encourages kids to know Jesus Christ and to grow in a relationship with Him. All parts of TeamKID—Bible stories, Bible verses, life application, missions, and recreation—connect to teach life lessons to kids.

The TeamKID motto is descriptive of what we try to accomplish:

Learning About God • Using the Bible • Living for Jesus

TeamKID helps preschoolers through a study of God's Word. Using fun activities and Bible material, kids can apply the Bible verses they learn to know how God wants them to live. A missions experience every week will open their eyes to the need of people around the world to hear about Jesus.

On the opposite side of this letter you will find a list of the topics we will be studying. We pray God will use these resources and our teaching to help your preschoolers apply these messages to their lives.

Sincerely,
The TeamKID Team

SESSION 1

THE PROMISE
THE BIBLE TELLS ABOUT JESUS.

Jesus is God's Son.
John 20:31

THIS WEEK'S BIBLE STORY: **God's Promised One**
(Genesis 1–3; Isaiah 7:10-14; 9:2-7; Micah 5:2; John 1:1-19)

WHAT'S INSIDE?

Match the pictures to the book that tells about them. Trace the word to see which Book tells us about Jesus.

TeamKID: Good News — PRESCHOOL ACTIVITY BOOK

PUT THE BOOKS IN ORDER

Draw a line from the book on the top shelf to the matching book on the bottom shelf. Trace the word from the book on the top shelf onto the book on the bottom shelf to learn one thing the Bible tells us about Jesus.

Your child is learning that the Bible tells us about Jesus. This week, help reinforce this truth with your child by reading verses from the Bible each day that tell about Jesus such as Isaiah 9:7; John 1:2; or John 20:31. Look up new verses every day to share.

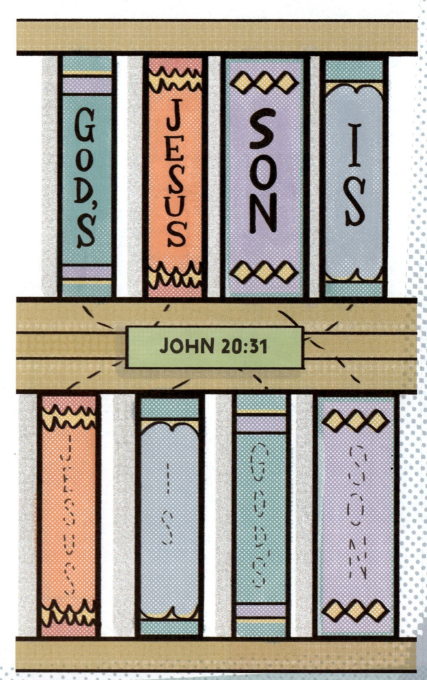

SESSION 2

THE FAMILY
GOD PLANNED A FAMILY FOR JESUS.

Jesus is God's Son.
John 20:31

THIS WEEK'S BIBLE STORY: The Family of Jesus
(Matthew 1:1-21; Luke 1:26-56; Luke 3, John 1:19)

GENERATION TO GENERATION
Trace the lines in the order of Jesus' family.

2 King David

3 Joseph and Mary

4 Baby Jesus

★ **1** Abraham

TeamKID: Good News — PRESCHOOL ACTIVITY BOOK

FAMILY PORTRAIT

Circle the number of people in your family.

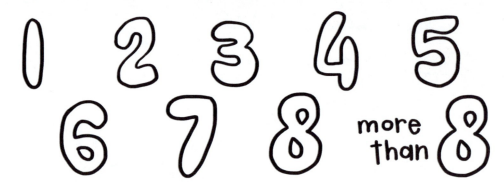

Draw a picture that includes the number of people you circled.

Your child is learning about the family God planned for Jesus to be a part of here on earth and that Jesus is God's Son. This week, help reinforce this truth with your child by talking about the family God planned for her. Pray over photographs of the people in your family with your child.

SESSION **3**

THE ARRIVAL
JESUS WAS BORN JUST LIKE GOD SAID.

Thank you, God, for Jesus.
Luke 2:38

THIS WEEK'S BIBLE STORY: The Birth & Boyhood of Jesus
(Luke 2)

NUMBER THE STORY

Help put the pictures in order. Draw a line to the number showing where each picture should go as it happened in the Bible story.

Simeon met Jesus

Shepherds visited Jesus

Jesus went to church

Jesus was born

1 2 3 4

TeamKID: Good News

LEARNING ABOUT JESUS

What are some ways you can learn about Jesus? Fill in the blanks by using one of these three pictures.

Going to ─────────────────

Reading the ─────────────────

Listening to my ─────────────────

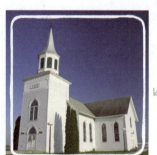

Your child is learning about how Jesus was born just like God said. This week, help reinforce this truth with your child by reading about Jesus' early life in Luke 2. Talk with your child about how he can learn more about Jesus.

SESSION **4**

THE MESSENGER
JOHN TOLD PEOPLE ABOUT JESUS.

John told people about Jesus.
Luke 3:18

THIS WEEK'S BIBLE STORY: John the Baptist
(Mark 1:1-8; John 1:19-28)

SEARCH FOR THE GOSPEL BOOKS
Cross out the letter Z. Circle the names of all four Gospel books.

MATTHEW   MARK   LUKE   JOHN

ZZZMATTHEWZ
ZZZZMARKZZZZ
ZZLUKEZZZZZZZ
ZZZZZJOHNZZZ

TeamKID: Good News

PRESCHOOL ACTIVITY BOOK **11**

I CAN TELL PEOPLE ABOUT JESUS

Trace your hand in the space below. Ask a parent or leader to write the names of people you can tell about Jesus on the fingers of your handprint.

Your child is learning about John the Baptist and how he told people about Jesus. This week, help reinforce this truth with your child by discussing the people around you who need to hear about Jesus. Talk about the truths you can share with them.

SESSION **5**

THE SON
JESUS IS GOD'S SON.

God said, "This is My Son; listen to Him."
Mark 9:7

THIS WEEK'S BIBLE STORY: Jesus Was Baptized
(Matthew 3:13-17)

COLOR BY NUMBER

Color the picture by number to reveal the message. Use the code below to match the number with the color.

1 🟡   2 🟢   3 🔴

TeamKID: Good News PRESCHOOL ACTIVITY BOOK **13**

FIND THE VERSE

Find and circle the words from today's Bible verse. Once you have found the words, fill in the verse below the picture.

"_____ said, 'This is my _____; listen to Him.'" _____ 9:7

Your child is learning that Jesus is God's Son and God wants us to listen to Him. This week, help reinforce this truth by talking about ways to listen to Jesus and do what He says.

SESSION 6

THE CALL
JESUS CHOSE HELPERS TO TELL PEOPLE THE GOOD NEWS.

Jesus chose helpers.
Mark 3:14

THIS WEEK'S BIBLE STORY: Jesus Called His First Disciples
(Luke 5:1-11)

JESUS' HELPERS

Count the helpers and write the number in the square. Trace the word to complete the Bible verse.

`12`

Here are the names of Jesus' disciples: Simon Peter, Andrew, James the son of Zebedee, John, Philip, Bartholomew, Thomas, Matthew, James, Thaddaeus, Simon, Judas Iscariot.

Jesus chose _HELPERS_.
Mark 3:14

TeamKID: Good News   PRESCHOOL ACTIVITY BOOK   15

WHERE CAN I TELL OTHERS ABOUT JESUS?

Decorate the word and circle the places you can talk to others about Jesus. Can you name other places you can tell about Jesus?

 playground    school

 ball field    home

Your child is learning that Jesus chose helpers to tell people the good news. This week, help your child know that we are Jesus' helpers, too. He wants us to tell others about Him. Talk with your child about people and places that she can tell others what she knows about Jesus.

SESSION 7: THE MINISTRY BEGINS
JESUS TOLD PEOPLE ABOUT GOD.

> Jesus told people the good news.
> Matthew 4:23

THIS WEEK'S BIBLE STORY: Jesus Began His Ministry
(Luke 4:14-30; Mark 1:35-38)

FINISH THE VERSE
Color the spaces marked with a ★ to complete the Bible verse.

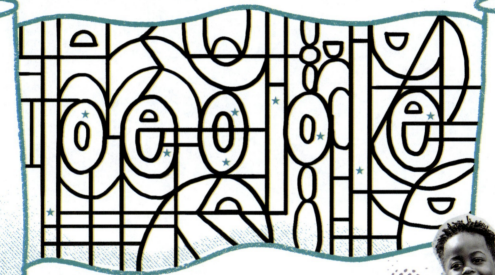

Jesus told [people] the good news.
Matthew 4:23

TeamKID: Good News

TELL PEOPLE THE
GOOD NEWS

Circle the people in the picture who need to hear the good news about Jesus.

Your child is learning that Jesus told people the good news. This week, help your child know that Jesus explained the words that were written about Him in the Bible. Read Isaiah 61:1-3 and talk about the good things God said Jesus would do.

SESSION 8

THE KINGDOM OF GOD
JESUS HELPS US KNOW HOW TO FOLLOW GOD'S PLAN.

Love other people and be kind.
Luke 6:27

THIS WEEK'S BIBLE STORY: The Sermon on the Mount (Matthew 5–7)

LOVE IS AN ACTION
Trace the heart around the pictures of people showing love and kindness.

WHERE CAN I SHOW LOVE AND BE KIND?

Draw a ✓ next to the places where you can show love and be kind to others.

AT HOME

Your child is learning that Jesus told people the good news. This week, talk about ways your family can show and tell people about Jesus and His love.

SESSION 9
THE WAY TO THE KINGDOM
GOD LOVED THE WORLD SO MUCH THAT HE SENT JESUS.

Jesus told people the good news.
Matthew 4:23

THIS WEEK'S BIBLE STORY: Jesus and Nicodemus (John 3)

NIGHTTIME VISIT
Trace the path leading Nicodemus to Jesus.

NICODEMUS

JESUS

HEART CONNECTION

Connect the hearts to place the Bible Truth in the correct order. Color each heart when you finish.

START

AT HOME

Your child is learning that God loves us so much that He sent Jesus. This week, reinforce this truth by reading John 3:16 to your child. For a challenge, work with your child to memorize the verse.

SESSION 10

THE HEALER

JESUS CAN DO THINGS NO ONE ELSE CAN DO.

Jesus made sick people well.
Luke 4:40

THIS WEEK'S BIBLE STORY: Jesus Healed and Restored
(Matthew 8:1-17; Luke 4:38-44)

CIRCLE THE FACES

Circle the faces that show how people might feel after they are healed by Jesus. In the face outline, draw how you would feel if Jesus healed one of your family members or friends.

TeamKID: Good News PRESCHOOL ACTIVITY BOOK 23

FIND THE PATH

Choose the path to help the man return to his son who has been healed by Jesus.

Your child is learning that Jesus can do things no one else can do. This week, help reinforce this truth with your child by reading stories from the Bible that tell about things only Jesus could do. Some examples include Matthew 8:5-13; Mark 7:31-37; Luke 8:22-25; Luke 17:11-19; and John 6:1-13.

SESSION 11

THE CREATOR
JESUS CAN DO THINGS NO ONE ELSE CAN DO.

Even the winds and the sea obey Him!
Matthew 8:27

THIS WEEK'S BIBLE STORY: Jesus Calmed the Storm
(Mark 4:35-41)

WHAT DOES NOT BELONG?
Circle the four objects that do not belong in the picture below.

TRACE THE VERSE
Review today's Bible verse as you trace the words.

Even the ____WINDS____ and the ____SEA____ obey ____HIM____!

Matthew 8:27

TeamKID: Good News   PRESCHOOL ACTIVITY BOOK   25

COLOR BY SHAPE

Use the shapes and color key to color the letters of Jesus' name. As you color, think of things Jesus can do that no one else can do.

 Your child is learning that Jesus can do things no one else can do. This week, help reinforce this truth with your child by reading the Bible story again. Talk about how God created the seas and winds and how He has power over all He has created.

SESSION 12

THE FORGIVER
JESUS CAN DO THINGS NO ONE ELSE CAN DO.

THIS WEEK'S BIBLE STORY: Jesus Forgave Sin
(Mark 2:1-17)

Jesus made sick people well. Luke 4:40

CONNECT THE SHAPES

"Get up, take your mat, and go home."

TeamKID: Good News · PRESCHOOL ACTIVITY BOOK · 27

CIRCLE THE PICTURES

The man in today's Bible story could not walk. He had friends who brought Him to Jesus. You may have friends today who cannot walk and may need your help. Circle the times below where you could help or include a friend who cannot walk.

Your child is learning that Jesus can do things no one else can do. This week, help reinforce this truth by reviewing the Bible story about the man who could not walk. Discuss what it might be like to not be able to use your legs, or how you could help a friend who could not use her legs. Talk about how the man must have felt and what he might have done after he was healed.

SESSION 13

THE COMPASSIONATE ONE
JESUS LOVES PEOPLE.

Jesus made sick people well.
Luke 4:40

THIS WEEK'S BIBLE STORY: Jesus Healed a Woman and Raised a Girl (Mark 5:21-43)

MATCH THE FACES

Jesus loves people. Look at the pictures below. Draw a line from the faces to the matching shadows.

TeamKID: Good News · PRESCHOOL ACTIVITY BOOK · 29

DRAW AND COLOR

Who does Jesus love? Draw a picture of people Jesus loves in the frame. (Remember—Jesus loves all people!) When you are finished, color the hearts around the frame using the number key.

1 Red   2 Yellow   3 Blue   4 Green

Your child is learning that Jesus loves people. This week, help reinforce this truth by talking about how Jesus loves everyone. It doesn't matter how old or young, whether you are a boy or a girl, or what color your skin is—Jesus loves people and shows compassion and kindness to them.

THE SENDER
PEOPLE AT CHURCH HELP OTHERS.

Jesus said, "Go and help others."
Luke 10:37

THIS WEEK'S BIBLE STORY: The Harvest and the Twelve
(Matthew 9:35–10:15)

TRACE THE LINES

Jesus wants people to tell others about Him. We can tell about Jesus wherever we go. Trace the lines from the people on the left side of the page to the items they may use on the right side of the page when they tell others about Jesus.

TeamKID: Good News PRESCHOOL ACTIVITY BOOK 31

GOING ON A JOURNEY

Jesus told the disciples what to bring with them on their journeys. Circle two things that the disciples would take with them.

Missionaries today also travel to tell people about Jesus. Draw a square around things today's missionaries might take with them on a journey.

Your child is learning that Jesus wants people to tell others about Him. This week, help reinforce this truth by naming people your family can tell about Jesus. Pray for these people and look for opportunities to share Jesus' love with them this week.

SESSION 15: THE ONE TO COME
NO MATTER WHAT HAPPENS, JESUS LOVES US.

Jesus said, "You are My friends." John 15:14

THIS WEEK'S BIBLE STORY: Jesus and John the Baptist (Matthew 11:1-14, 25-28, Luke 7:18-30)

CONNECT AND TRACE

The Bible teaches us about Jesus. We learn that Jesus loves us and calls us His friends. Connect the dots to finish the Bible. Then, trace the Bible verse reference where we can read that we are friends of Jesus.

Each Bible verse has a book name, a chapter number, and a verse number. Ask a grown-up to help you find John 15:14 in a Bible.

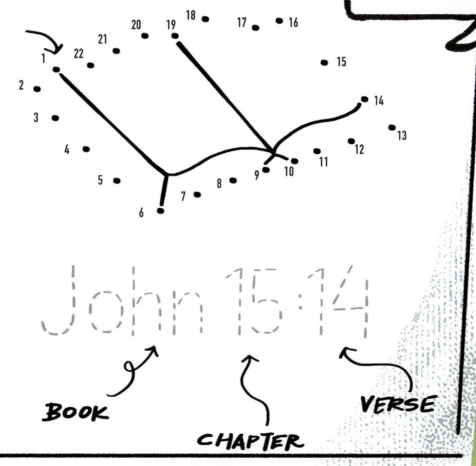

TeamKID: Good News

MATCH THE MIRACLE

Even John the Baptist, a friend and follower of Jesus, sometimes needed reassurance that Jesus truly is the Son of God. Jesus reminded John of the miracles only He could do. Match the before and after pictures of some of Jesus' miracles.

Your child is learning that no matter what happens, Jesus loves us. This week, help reinforce this truth by reminding your preschooler that followers of Jesus sometimes have questions about whether or not Jesus truly is the Son of God. Share that as you read God's Word, you can know that Jesus is God's Son, the Savior of the world.

SESSION 16

THE LAWGIVER
JESUS IS GOD'S SON AND LOVES PEOPLE.

Love God and love others.
Luke 10:27

THIS WEEK'S BIBLE STORY: Jesus Healed on the Sabbath
(Matthew 12:1-14)

CIRCLE THE PICTURES

Luke 10:27 reminds us to love God and love others. Look at the pictures. Circle the pictures that show ways kids can show love to others.

SPOT THE DIFFERENCES

No matter what shape, size, or color, Jesus loves people! Look at the pictures below. Can you spot the differences in each pair? (Hint: there are 7 total!)

Your child is learning that Jesus is God's Son and loves people. This week, help reinforce this truth by discussing ways Jesus showed love to people. Share ways your family can show love to others. Try to do at least one of these things this week.

SESSION 17

THE SOWER
JESUS HELPS ME KNOW HOW TO FOLLOW GOD'S PLAN.

Jesus grew and became wise.
Luke 2:52

THIS WEEK'S BIBLE STORY: The Parable of the Sower
(Luke 8:4-15)

FIND THE BIBLES

As we read God's Word, we learn about God's plans for us. Look at the picture below. Circle the 6 hidden Bibles as you find them.

TeamKID: Good News

PRESCHOOL ACTIVITY BOOK 37

PUT THE PICTURES IN ORDER

Today's Bible verse says, "Jesus grew and became wise." Just like we grow from a baby into a grown-up, Jesus did the same. Look at the pictures of the people. Put the pictures in order by drawing a line from the youngest person to number 1 all the way to the oldest person to number 4.

Your child is learning that Jesus helps him know how to follow God's plan. This week, help reinforce this truth by reading the parable of the sower. Talk about the importance of having "good soil" for God's Word to take root. As a reminder of this story, plant a seed and watch it grow over the next few weeks.

SESSION 18

THE SON OF GOD

JESUS IS GOD'S SON. HE CAN DO THINGS NO ONE ELSE CAN DO.

Jesus is God's Son.
John 20:31

THIS WEEK'S BIBLE STORY: Jesus Fed 5,000 and Walked on Water (John 6:1-59)

COLOR AND TRACE

Matthew, Mark, Luke, and John are known as the Gospel books of the Bible. Color the books on the bookshelf. Then, trace the words to reveal one thing we learn about Jesus in these books.

The Gospels teach us JESUS IS GOD'S SON.

TeamKID: Good News

CIRCLE THE PICTURES

When Jesus fed 5,000 people, He didn't have a grocery store to stop at on the way. What did Jesus use to feed the people? Circle the pictures that Jesus used to feed the people. Draw an X over the things Jesus did not use.

Your child is learning that Jesus is God's Son. He can do things no one else can do. This week, help reinforce this truth by reading about the miracles of Jesus feeding 5,000 and Jesus walking on water. Talk about different things Jesus can do that no one else can do. Help your child see that Jesus is different from anyone who has ever lived. He is God's Son.

SESSION 19

THE PROMISED ONE
JESUS IS THE ONE GOD PROMISED.

Peter said, "You are the Son of God."
Matthew 16:16

THIS WEEK'S BIBLE STORY: Jesus Is the Messiah
(Matthew 16:13-28; Mark 8:27-30; Luke 9:18-27)

COUNT THE PEOPLE

Count the people in each picture. Write the number below the picture.

3   5   2

4   1

Jesus is the __ONE__ God promised.

TeamKID: Good News — PRESCHOOL ACTIVITY BOOK — 41

WHO IS JESUS?

Use the code to help tell who Jesus is.

Jesus is the **S O N** of **G O D**

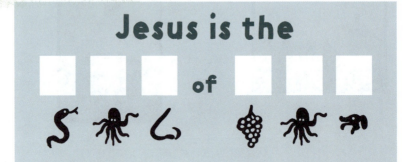

Your child is learning that Jesus is God's Son, the One God promised to send. This week reinforce this truth by looking for and counting things God made. Point out that Jesus is God's One and only Son and that He is the One God promised to send.

SESSION 20

THE MERCIFUL NEIGHBOR
JESUS TAUGHT US TO BE KIND TO OTHERS.

Love other people and be kind.
Luke 6:27

THIS WEEK'S BIBLE STORY: The Parable of the Good Samaritan
(Luke 10:25-37)

Show Love to Others

Trace the lines around the pictures of someone showing love to others. Draw an X through the pictures that do not show love.

HELPING HAND

Follow the path the Samaritan man took to Jericho. Each time you come to a letter, copy it into the blanks to complete the Bible verse to discover how God wants us to treat others.

__LOVE__ other people and be __KIND__.

Luke 6:27

Your child is learning that Jesus taught us to be kind to others. This week reinforce this truth by helping your child show love and kindness to others in your home. Talk with her about things she can do to follow what Jesus taught such as helping her brother clean up his toys.

SESSION 21

THE LOST ARE FOUND
JESUS LOVES ME, SO I AM SPECIAL.

Jesus loves you.
John 15:12

THIS WEEK'S BIBLE STORY: The Lost Sheep, Coin, and Son
(Luke 15; Matthew 18:10-14)

LOOK AND FIND
Find and circle the items in the picture.

SELF-PORTRAIT

Draw a picture of yourself in the frame below.

JESUS LOVES... _____,

SO I AM SPECIAL.

Your child is learning that because Jesus loves him, he is special. Reinforce this truth by noting things about your child that make him special.

THE FIRST ARE LAST
JESUS FORGIVES AND SO SHOULD WE.

SESSION 22

Jesus said, "Love one another." John 15:17

THIS WEEK'S BIBLE STORY: The Unforgiving Servant (Matthew 18:21-35)

COLOR BY NUMBER
Use the number and color key to color the letters to discover one thing Jesus wants us to do.

TeamKID: Good News — PRESCHOOL ACTIVITY BOOK — 47

HOW MANY TIMES?

Count how many times you can do each action in 15 seconds. Ask a friend or a grown-up to keep time.

Hop on one foot. ☐

Pat your head. ☐

Clap your hands. ☐

Jesus wants us to forgive others every time.

AT HOME

Your child is learning that because Jesus forgives her, she should also forgive others. This week help your kids ask others to forgive them when they do something wrong and to forgive others when they are wronged. Here are a few more verses to read together about forgiveness; Matthew 6:14; Ephesians 4:32; and Colossians 3:13.

SESSION **23**

THE POOR ARE RICH
DON'T WORRY. GOD TAKES CARE OF US.

Jesus said, "Do not worry. God will take care of you."
Luke 12:22,24

THIS WEEK'S BIBLE STORY: Possessions and the Kingdom of God
(Luke 12:13-34)

WHAT DO YOU NEED?

Circle the pictures of the things you need. Draw a square around the pictures of things you might want but don't need.

COLOR AND DISCOVER

Color all the letters except the Xs to remember what Jesus said.

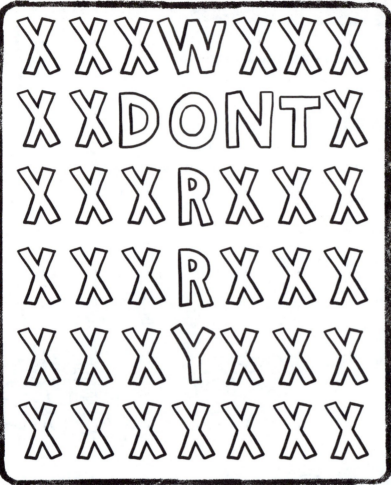

AT HOME

Jesus said, "Do not worry. God will take care of you." Luke 12:22,24

Your child is learning that he does not have to worry because God takes care of us. Reinforce this truth with your child by talking to him about the things he may worry about. Stop and say a prayer of praise each time God provides something that your family needs or is worried about.

SESSION 24
THE GENEROUS KING
**JESUS LOVES EVERYONE.
I CAN LOVE LIKE JESUS.**

Jesus said, "Love others as I love you."
John 13:34

THIS WEEK'S BIBLE STORY: The Vineyard Workers (Matthew 20:1-16)

WHO DOES JESUS SAY TO LOVE?
Color the land green and the water blue. Trace the letters to discover who Jesus says we should love.

TeamKID: Good News

PRESCHOOL ACTIVITY BOOK 51

FINISH THE FRAMES

Color each frame. Talk about how you can love the people in the frames.

AT HOME

Your child is learning that Jesus loves everyone and so should she. Reinforce this truth by helping her show love to everyone. Point out the different people you meet at the store, at church, or other places you visit and remind your child Jesus loves everyone.

THE KINGDOM IS FOR EVERYONE

JESUS TAUGHT THAT WE SHOULD LOVE EVERYONE.

Jesus said, "Love others as you love yourself." Mark 12:31

THIS WEEK'S BIBLE STORY: The Wedding Banquet (Matthew 22:1-14)

SET THE TABLE
Connect the dots to complete the picture.

PARTY INVITATION

The king in the story invited people to a celebration. Pretend that you are having a party. Decorate the invitation below. Who would you invite to your party?

Your child is learning that Jesus taught that we should love everyone. Reinforce this concept by planning a special meal or banquet. Invite friends or family who need to know about God's kingdom. Encourage your child to share the things he is learning about Jesus and how He loves everyone.

SESSION 26: THE REWARDS OF THE KINGDOM

WE NEED TO LOVE AND SERVE OTHERS.

THIS WEEK'S BIBLE STORY: The Greatest Will Serve (Matthew 20:20-28; Mark 10:35-45)

Jesus said, "Love others as you love yourself." Mark 12:31

SERVE OTHERS

Draw a line from the item to the picture of the person using it to serve someone.

TeamKID: Good News — PRESCHOOL ACTIVITY BOOK

COMPLETE THE VERSE

Follow the arrows to color the words to complete the Bible verse.

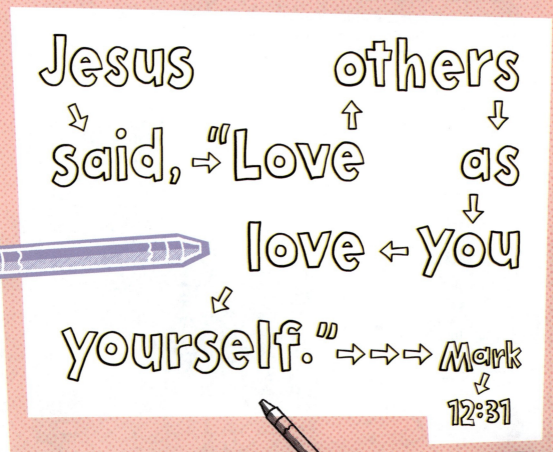

AT HOME

Your child is learning that Jesus wants us to love and serve others. Reinforce this truth by looking for ways to love and serve others. Suggest your children put this into practice as they are playing with their siblings or friends by allowing them to go first.

SESSION 27: WAITING FOR THE KINGDOM

WE CAN SHOW GOD WE LOVE HIM BY USING WHAT HE GIVES US TO SERVE HIM.

> Do those things that are pleasing to God.
> 1 John 3:22

THIS WEEK'S BIBLE STORY: Showing God's Love by Helping Others (Matthew 25:35-40)

DO WHAT PLEASES GOD

Draw in a happy face below the pictures showing the things that please God and a sad face below the things that do not.

TeamKID: Good News — PRESCHOOL ACTIVITY BOOK

COMPLETE THE PATTERN

Look at the pattern in each row and circle the picture that completes the pattern. How was each item used to serve others in the Bible story?

AT HOME

Your child is learning that he can show love by doing things that are pleasing to God and using the things he has to serve Him. Reinforce this truth by providing opportunities for your family to serve others such as giving to a food bank, distributing water at a local park, and so forth.

SESSION 28
THE ANOINTING
I CAN SHOW JESUS I LOVE HIM.

Thank You, God, for Jesus.
Luke 2:38

THIS WEEK'S BIBLE STORY: Jesus Was Anointed (John 12:1-8)

COMPLETE THE MAZE
Find your way through the maze by passing through each picture. Each picture shows a different way you can show Jesus you love Him.

COLOR BY NUMBER

Use the number and color key to color the hearts. As you color, think about ways you can show Jesus you love Him.

1 — red
2 — orange
3 — yellow
4 — green
5 — purple

AT HOME

Your child is learning that he can show Jesus he loves Him. This week, help reinforce this truth by discussing ways your family can show love to Jesus. Choose a different way to show love to Jesus each day. This could include praying, singing, serving, and giving.

SESSION 29

THE KING
PEOPLE WELCOMED JESUS TO JERUSALEM.

Children cheered, "Hosanna" when they saw Jesus.
Matthew 21:15

THIS WEEK'S BIBLE STORY: Jesus Entered Jerusalem
(Luke 19:28-44; Matthew 21:1-11; Mark 11:1-11; John 12:12-19)

FIND THE HIDDEN PICTURES
Can you find the 4 objects hidden in the picture? Look closely! The items are hidden two times!

answer key

TeamKID: Good News

PRESCHOOL ACTIVITY BOOK 61

CIRCLE THE PICTURES

Jesus traveled into Jerusalem riding a donkey. Today we can travel to tell others about Jesus so they can know about Him. Circle the pictures that show ways we can travel to share the good news of Jesus to others.

Your child is learning that people welcomed Jesus to Jerusalem. This week, help reinforce this truth with your child by reading each of the passages listed above throughout the week. As you think about Jesus' last week on earth, spend time worshiping Jesus as the Savior of the world.

SESSION 30
THE LAST SUPPER
JESUS SHOWED HIS HELPERS HOW TO HELP OTHERS.

Jesus said, "Do for others like I have done for you."
John 13:15

THIS WEEK'S BIBLE STORY: The Last Supper
(Matthew 26:17-30; Mark 14:1-26; Luke 22:14-23; John 13:1-20)

MATCH THE FEET

Jesus shared a special meal with His disciples. At this meal, Jesus washed the feet of His friends. Look at the feet below. Draw a line from each foot to its match.

TRACE YOUR FOOT

In the blank space below, have a grown-up help you trace your foot. Decorate it with crayons. Use this drawing as a reminder to obey John 13:15:

"Do for others like I have done for you."

AT HOME

Your child is learning about a special meal Jesus had with His disciples before He died. At this meal, Jesus showed His helpers how to help others. This week, help reinforce this truth with your child by talking about ways he can help others. Choose one or two ways your family can show love to others this week.

64 PRESCHOOL ACTIVITY BOOK   TeamKID: Good News

GOD'S KINGDOM HAS COME
JESUS FOLLOWED GOD'S PLAN FOR HIM.

SESSION 31

> Jesus talked to God.
> John 17:1

THIS WEEK'S BIBLE STORY: Jesus Prayed in the Garden
(Luke 22:39–46; Matthew 26:36-46; Mark 14:32-42)

CIRCLE THE PLACES

Jesus prayed in many places. Look at the pictures below. Circle the place where Jesus prayed in the Bible story. Draw a square around places where you can pray.

DRAW PICTURES

In each box below, draw one thing you can pray for. Remember that just like Jesus talked to God, you can talk to God about anything.

I can talk to God!

Your child is learning how Jesus followed God's plan for Him, even when it was hard. This week, help reinforce this truth with your child by talking about what it means to follow God's plan. Share examples from your own life when you have followed God's plan, even when it was hard.

SESSION 32: THE KING OF KINGS
JESUS IS ALIVE!

Jesus is alive! Matthew 28:7

THIS WEEK'S BIBLE STORY: Jesus' Death and Resurrection (Luke 24:1-12; Matthew 28:1-10; Mark 16:1-13; John 20:1-23)

COLOR THE CROSS

Easter is a special time we celebrate the fact that Jesus is alive! He died on a cross, and three days later He rose from the dead. We can praise God because Jesus is alive!

WHAT'S WRONG WITH THIS PICTURE?

Look at the picture of Mary at the empty tomb. What is wrong with it? Circle 5 things that do not belong.

AT HOME

Your child is learning about one of the greatest events that has ever taken place—Jesus' resurrection. Your child is learning that Jesus is alive! This week, help reinforce this truth with your child by reading the Bible passages listed. Spend time thanking God that Jesus is not dead—He is alive!

SESSION 33

THE PROMISE KEPT
JESUS IS ALIVE! JUST AS HE PROMISED!

Jesus is God's Son.
John 20:31

THIS WEEK'S BIBLE STORY: Jesus Is Alive
(Luke 24:1-12; Matthew 28:1-10; Mark 16:1-13; John 20:1-23)

SORT THE PICTURES

Jesus is alive! Just as He promised! When Jesus died on the cross, He was no longer living. But, He didn't stay there! He rose from the grave! Jesus is alive! Circle the pictures below that show things that are living. Place an X over the pictures that show things that are not living.

TeamKID: Good News

FIND THE RIGHT PATH

When Mary told the disciples that Jesus was alive, two of the disciples ran to see if the tomb was really empty. Follow the paths below to see which group of men made it to the empty tomb.

Your child is learning that Jesus is alive, just as He promised! This week, help reinforce this truth with your child by talking about what it means to keep a promise. Think of different things the Bible promises to us. Remind your child that God ALWAYS keeps His promises!

SESSION 34
THE PROMISE FULFILLED
THE WHOLE BIBLE TELLS ABOUT JESUS.

The Bible is true.
John 17:17

THIS WEEK'S BIBLE STORY: Jesus Appeared to His Disciples
(Luke 24:13-49; John 20:24-30)

FIND THE DIFFERENT SCROLL
In Bible times, people read from Bible scrolls. They did not have Bibles like we have today. Look at the scrolls below. Circle the scroll that is different in each row.

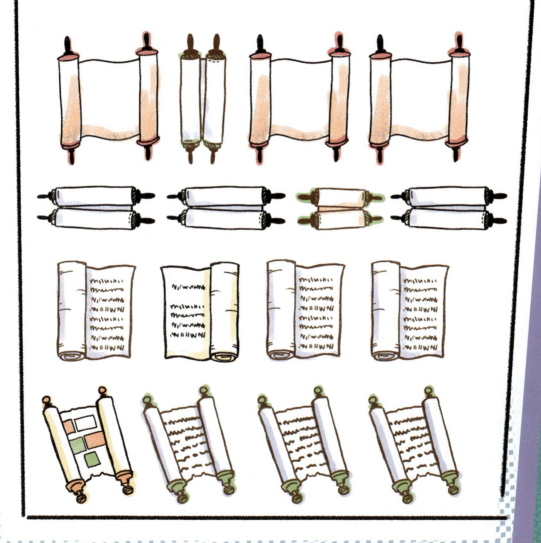

EXPLORE YOUR BIBLE

The whole Bible tells about Jesus. Because we learn about Jesus as we read the Bible, it is important to be able to use it. Find a Bible at your home. Work with a grown-up to answer the questions below by circling yes or no. (If you don't have a Bible at home, please let your TeamKID leader know!)

1. Does your Bible have pictures? ☐ yes ☐ no

2. Can you find the first page of your Bible? ☐ yes ☐ no

3. Can you find the last page of your Bible? ☐ yes ☐ no

4. Does your Bible have maps? (Hint: Look in the back!) ☐ yes ☐ no

5. Does your Bible have black words and red words in it? (Red words help us know what Jesus said. In some Bibles, His words are printed in red.) ☐ yes ☐ no

6. Does your Bible have an Old Testament and a New Testament? ☐ yes ☐ no

AT HOME

Your child is learning that we can learn about Jesus as we read the Bible. The whole Bible tells about Jesus. This week, help reinforce this truth with your child by reminding her from the book of Genesis to the book of Revelation, the Bible points us to truths about Jesus. Look through an illustrated children's Bible or a storybook Bible to see some of these amazing stories.

SESSION 35

THE RESTORATION
JESUS WILL ALWAYS LOVE ME.

THIS WEEK'S BIBLE STORY: Jesus Forgives and Restores (John 21)

> Yes, Jesus, you know that I love you.
> John 21:16

WRITE YOUR NAME

Write your name on the line. Ask a grown-up if you need help. Remember that Jesus will always love you. Use crayons to decorate the space around your name.

Jesus will always love
_____

COLOR THE FISH

Jesus helped the disciples (helpers) catch many fish by telling them to cast their nets on the other side of their boat. Color the picture below.

4 red fish
3 blue fish
2 green fish
1 yellow fish

AT HOME

Your child is learning that Jesus will always love him. No matter what your child does, there is nothing that could take away Jesus' love for him. This week, help reinforce this truth with your child by reminding him that just like you love him, Jesus' love for him is even greater than that. Search for a few songs that talk about loving Jesus. Listen to and sing them together this week.

SESSION 36
THE PROMISE CONTINUED
WE CAN TELL OTHERS ABOUT JESUS.

Go and tell others about Jesus.
Matthew 28:19-20

THIS WEEK'S BIBLE STORY: The Great Commission
(Luke 24:50-53; Matthew 28:16-20; Mark 16:14-20)

CIRCLE THE PICTURES

We can talk to people in many different ways using many different things to spread the good news of Jesus to the world. Circle the pictures below that show things you can use to tell others about Jesus.

TeamKID: Good News

PRESCHOOL ACTIVITY BOOK 75

MY PRAYER LIST

Ask a grown-up to help you write a list of people you want to tell about Jesus. Tear this page out and put it in a place where it can remind you to pray for each one.

Your child is learning that we can tell others about Jesus. This is the very last commandment Jesus gave His disciples. This week, help reinforce this truth with your child by thinking of a few people you can tell about Jesus together. Find at least one way to tell one of these people about Jesus this week.

BONUS 1

WHO IS JESUS?
THE BIBLE TELLS US ABOUT JESUS, GOD'S SON

Jesus said, "The Bible tells about Me."
John 5:39

THIS WEEK'S BIBLE STORY: The Jesus of the Gospels
(John 1:1-18; John 20:30-31; Luke 1:1-4; Mark 1:1; Matthew 1:1)

SEARCH FOR THE BIBLES
Circle all the Bibles in the picture.

JESUS SAID, "The Bible tells about Me." John 5:39

TeamKID: Good News — PRESCHOOL ACTIVITY BOOK

WHO IS JESUS?

Talk about the pictures that show who the Bible says Jesus is and what He does. Trace the word in the phrase below the last picture.

Jesus is God's ⎯SON⎯ .

Your child is learning who the Bible says Jesus is. This week, help reinforce this concept by reading about one of Jesus' miracles in the book of John. Point out to your child that Jesus can do things no one else can because He is God's Son.

BONUS 2

THE SHEPHERDS WORSHIPED JESUS
JESUS WAS BORN JUST LIKE GOD PROMISED.

Jesus was born in Bethlehem.
Luke 2:11

THIS WEEK'S BIBLE STORY: Jesus Was Born (Luke 2)

COUNT THE SHEEP

Angels appeared to shepherds to tell them about the birth of Jesus. A shepherd's job was to take care of sheep. Count the number of sheep in the picture. Circle the number of sheep you find.

1 2 3 4 5

COLOR THE PICTURE

Jesus was born just like God promised. Color the picture below. Hang it in your home to help you remember the true meaning of Christmas.

AT HOME

Your child is learning that Jesus was born just like God promised. This week, help reinforce this truth by reading Luke 2 with your child. Talk with him about the true meaning of Christmas—God sent His Son, Jesus, to earth as a baby. He lived on earth, did things no one else can do, and then died on the cross to save us from our sins. Jesus is now in heaven and will return one day.

JESUS IS ALIVE
THE WHOLE BIBLE TELLS ABOUT JESUS.

Jesus said, "The Bible is true and tells about Me."
Luke 24:44

THIS WEEK'S BIBLE STORY: The Emmaus Disciples (Luke 24:13-35)

ALIVE OR NOT?

Use the code below to find out who the men talked to on the road to Emmaus.

TRACE THE BIBLE

Trace the Bible and color it in. Color the word True inside the Bible. The Bible is true and tells about **Jesus**!

Your child is learning that the Bible is true and tells about Jesus. Reinforce this truth by going on a walk with her. As you walk, discuss things that the Bible tells about Jesus. Remind your child that everything the Bible says is true.

THE MISSION OF THE KINGDOM

BONUS 4

I CAN TELL OTHERS THE GOOD NEWS THAT JESUS LOVES THEM.

Jesus said, "I love you." John 15:9

THIS WEEK'S BIBLE STORY: Peter Preached at Pentecost (Acts 2)

COLOR THE PEOPLE

Color the people below. As you color, think of who you can tell about Jesus.

READ THE STORY

Work with a grown-up to read this story. When you see a picture instead of a word, name the picture as you read.

I can tell the good news that Jesus  them. Jesus  the whole . Jesus is the Savior of the . Because Jesus  me, I can share this good news with everywhere.

REBUS KEY

 people

 loves

 world

Your child is learning that it is important to tell others the good news that Jesus loves them. This week, help reinforce this truth with your child by talking about how Jesus loves the world. Name a few ways you know Jesus loves you. Then, think of a few people who need to hear this good news.

THE GOSPEL
GOD'S PLAN FOR PRESCHOOLERS

gos·pel [noun.] good news; the message about Christ, the kingdom of God, and salvation

GOD IS KING.
Ask: "Who is in charge at home? Who is in charge over the whole world?" Explain that God made everything! He is King over everything, and He is in charge.

WE SINNED.
Ask: "Have you ever done something wrong?" Tell preschoolers that everyone sins, or disobeys God. Our sin makes God sad.

GOD SENT JESUS.
Explain that God must punish sin. He loves us, and He sent His Son, Jesus, to earth. Jesus came to take away the punishment for sin.

JESUS LOVES.
Ask: "Do you like presents?" Explain that Jesus gives us the best present. He never did anything wrong, but He was punished in our place. Jesus wants to take away our sin because He loves us.

As you faithfully teach the Bible, you are planting gospel seeds in children's hearts. Ask God to grow the preschoolers into children who love and trust in Jesus.

FAMILY DEVOTIONS

Help your preschoolers love and remember Bible stories as well as they remember their favorite bedtime books. While you won't get your kids to sit still for 20 minutes, you can capture their attention for 5. Here are some tips to get you started.

- ☐ Plan for it, or it won't happen. Know when and where you'll do it.
- ☐ Keep your resources in the same place and ready to go. Delaying a routine even by 20 seconds can make it harder to maintain.
- ☐ Be consistent. Hold each other accountable to do it. (Many times, your kids will help with this!)
- ☐ Break your stories into smaller pieces. Preschoolers have a short attention span and limited understanding. Tell the Bible story in preschool-friendly language.
- ☐ Plan ahead of time. Don't just open your Bible to a section and decide "this is where we're going to read tonight." Choose Bible stories and help kids apply these truths to their lives.
- ☐ Lower your expectations. It's just not always going to be a "special, deep" moment. But it will get better! Some action is better than nothing!
- ☐ Make your routine less "routine." Preschoolers learn best by doing. Incorporate that knowledge into your devotion time. Be creative! Below are some tips to get you started.
  - ☐ Teach through games. (For example: "Follow the Leader" teaches obedience—a good point to make when talking about Noah's obedience to God).
  - ☐ Make a photo album of people to pray for.
  - ☐ Act out the Bible story.
  - ☐ Color a picture while someone reads the story. (Kids often learn better when their hands are busy.)

> "Imprint these words of mine on your hearts and minds, bind them as a sign on your hands, and let them be a symbol on your foreheads. Teach them to your children, talking about them when you sit in your house and when you walk along the road, when you lie down and when you get up. Write them on the doorposts of your house and on your city gates, so that as long as the heavens are above the earth, your days and those of your children may be many in the land the LORD swore to give your ancestors."
>
> Deuteronomy 11:18-21

PRESCHOOL BIBLE SKILLS

Below are Bible Skills that TeamKID can help your preschooler attain. Note that all children are different and learn at different paces. Your child can continue to master these skills as you work with him at home.

- ☐ Know everything in the Bible is true.
- ☐ Understand that the Bible teaches us what God and Jesus are like.
- ☐ Learn that God told people what to write in the Bible.
- ☐ Hear that the Bible teaches that Jesus lived on earth, died on the cross, God made Him live again, and He is now in heaven.
- ☐ Hear that the Bible teaches people how God wants them to live.
- ☐ Know that there are two main parts of the Bible—the Old Testament and the New Testament.
- ☐ Begin to understand that a Bible reference includes a book, chapter, and reference. Open the Bible to a specifically marked verse in the Bible.
- ☐ Remember and say simple Bible words, phrases, and verses with Bible references.
- ☐ Remember and retell a familiar Bible story or Bible fact.
- ☐ Begin to understand how Bible verses apply to life.
- ☐ Use the Bible at home with family members.
- ☐ Name a few Bible books in order.
- ☐ Learn how to tell others about God and Jesus.

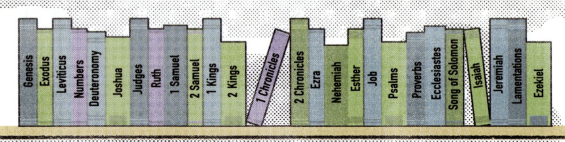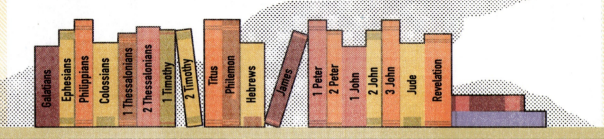